Old-Fashioned Fairy Tales.

*WITH TWELVE ORIGINAL DESIGNS BY A. W. BAYES AND GORDON BROWNE,
AND OTHER ILLUSTRATIONS.*

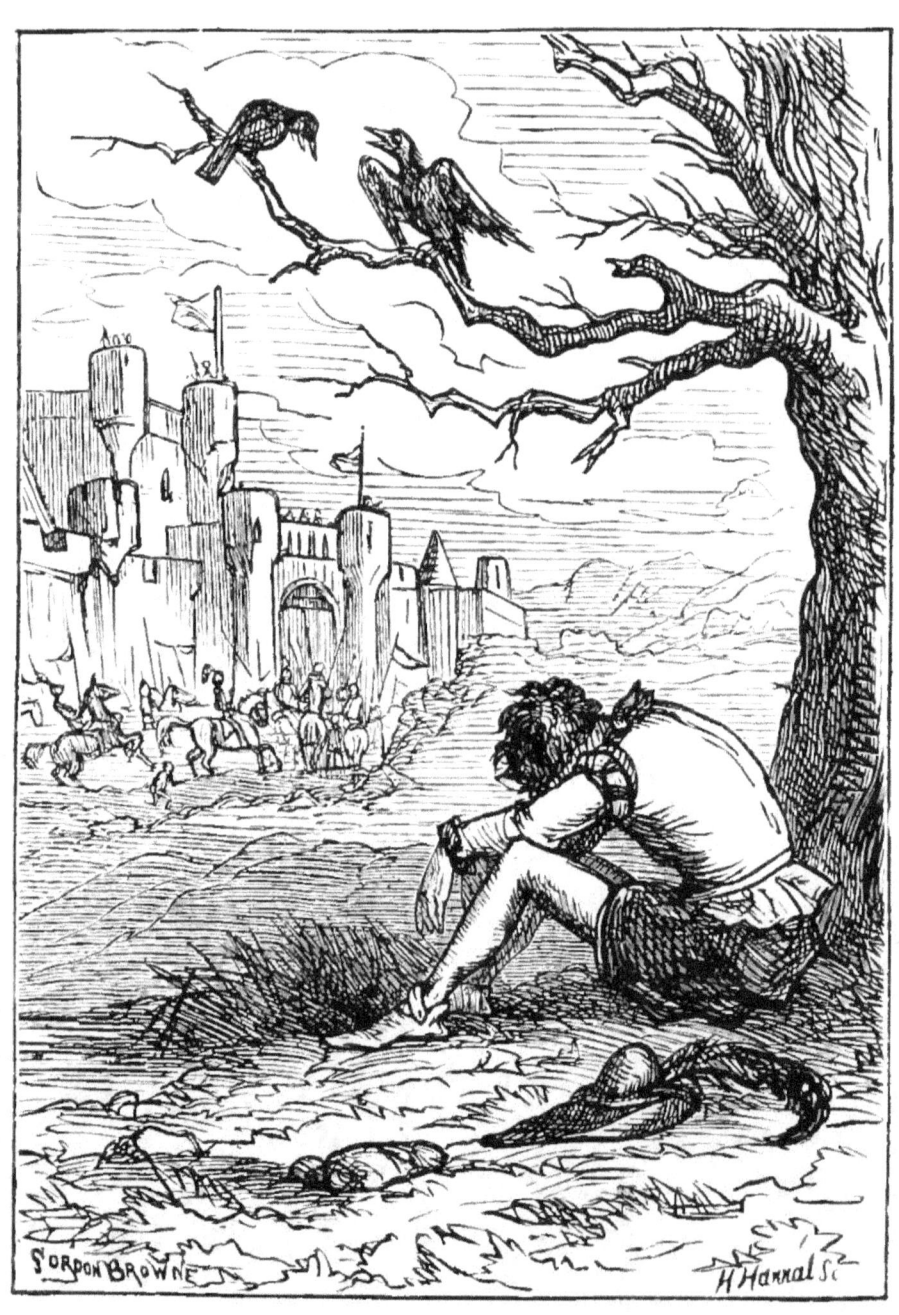

"*He heard the birds talking above him.*"

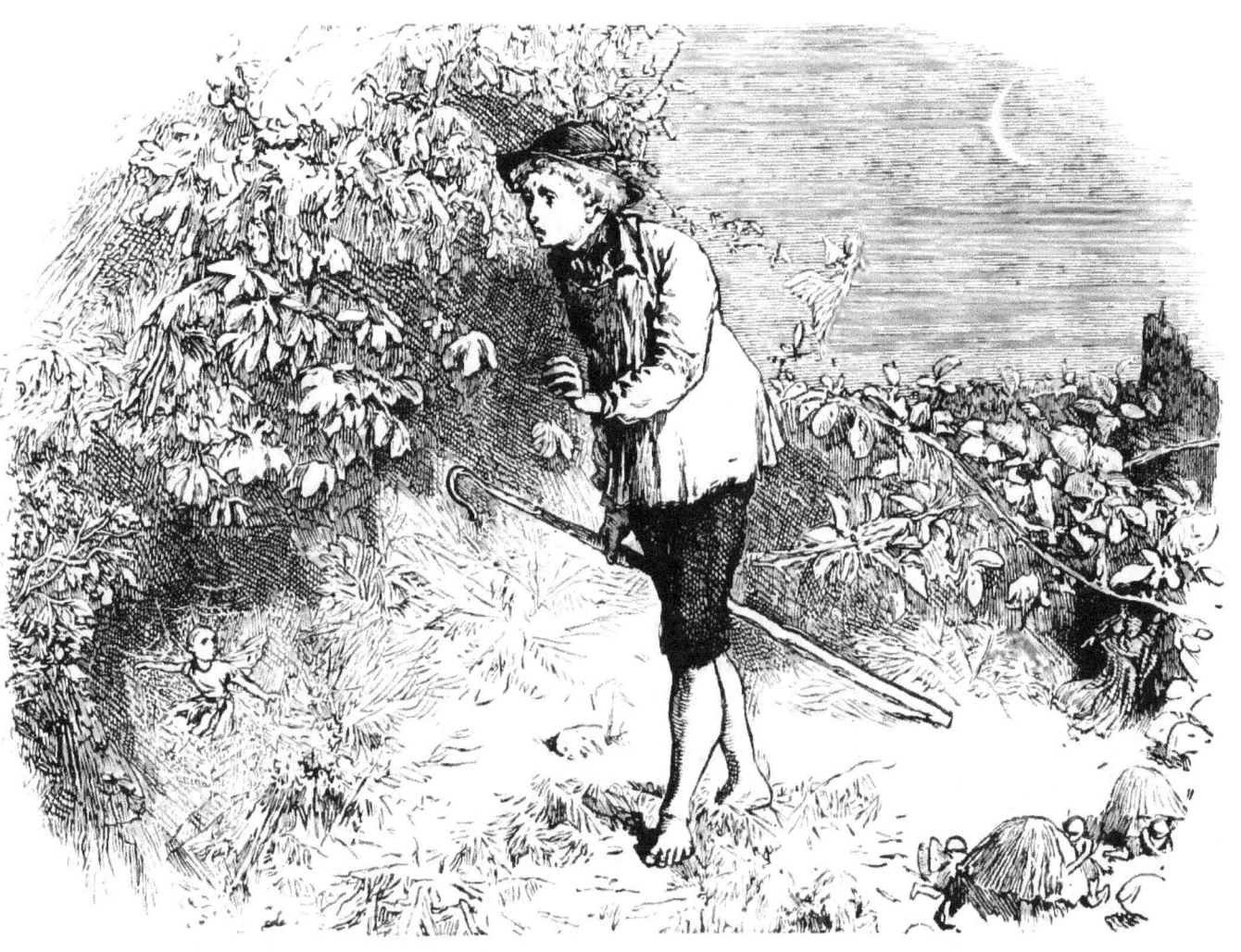

"Know'st thou not the little path
That winds about the Ferny brae?
That is the road to bonnie Elfland,
Where thou and I this night maun gae."
                    THOS. THE RHYMER.

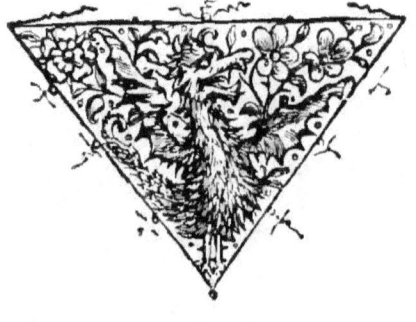

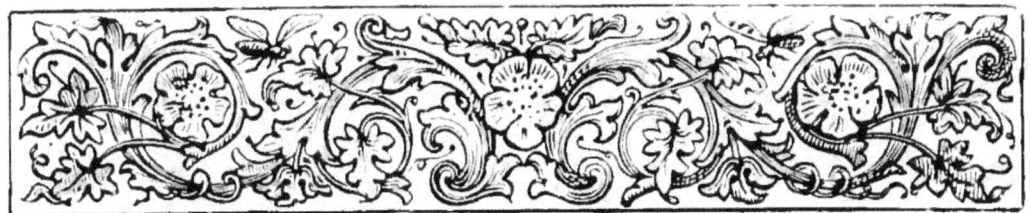

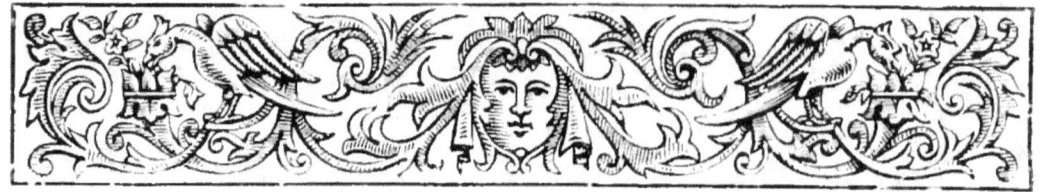

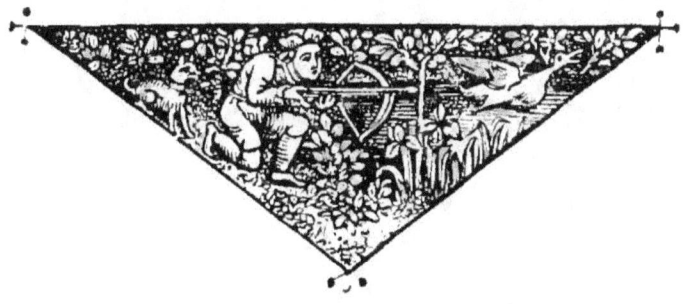

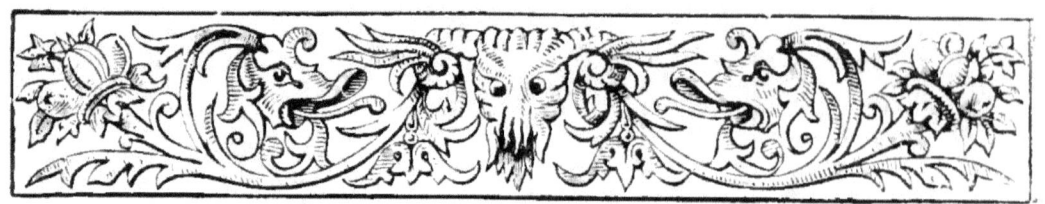

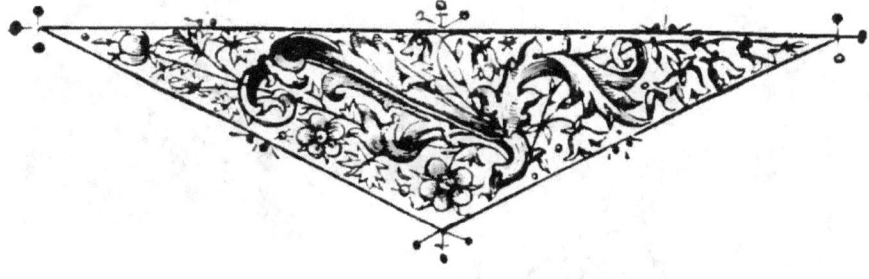

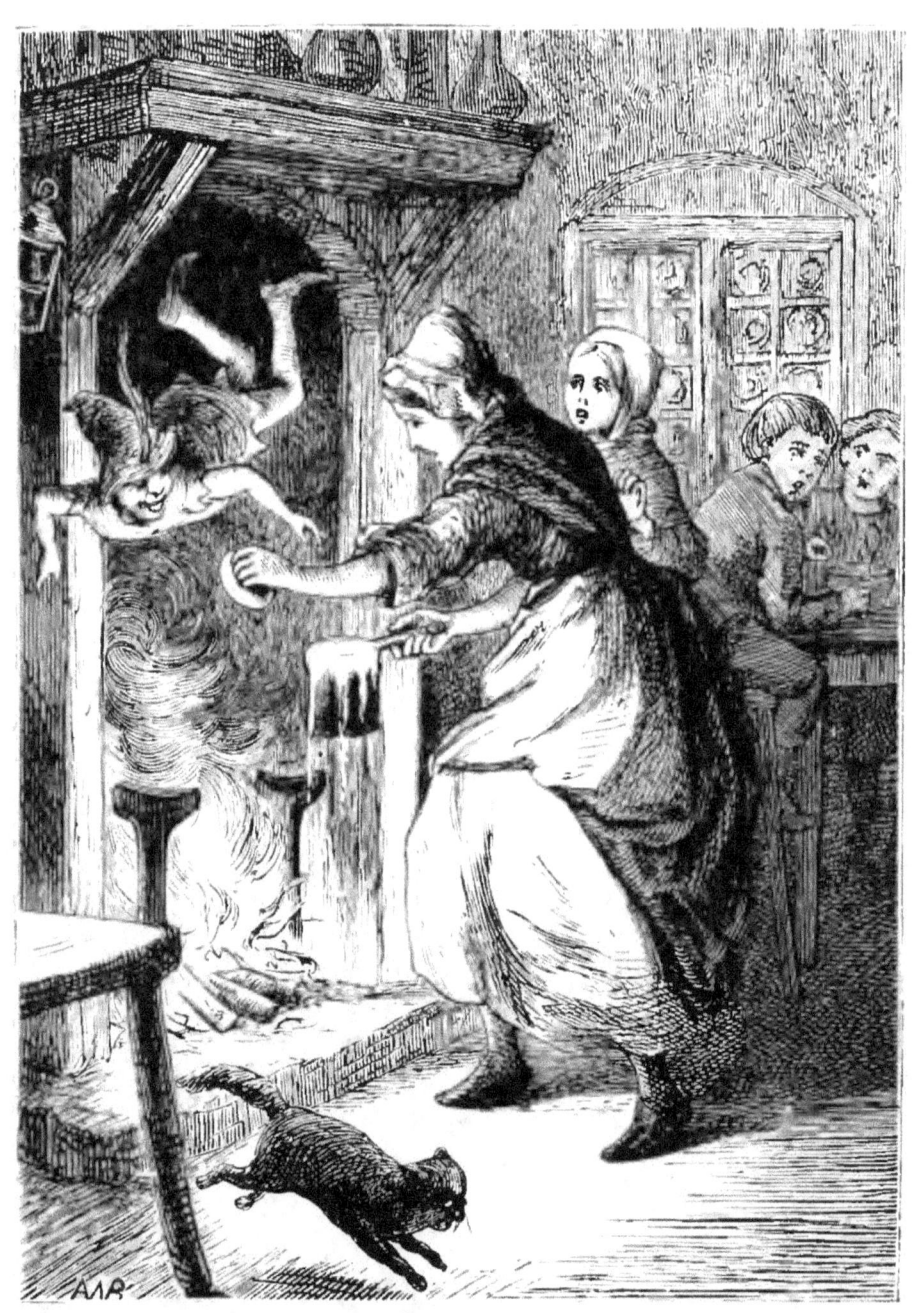

"*The Hillman himself came tumbling down the chimney.*"

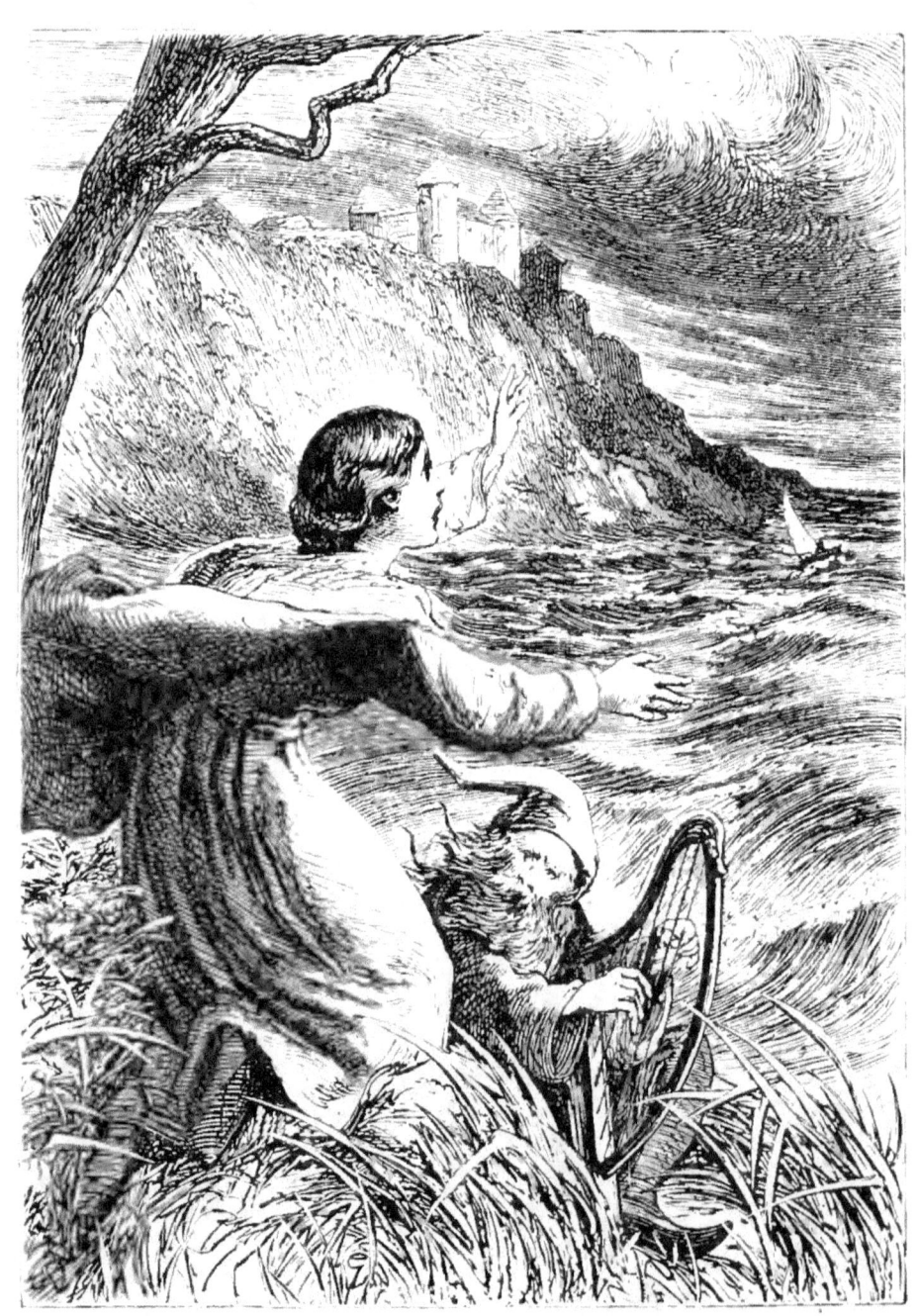

"They say, 'When Necks play, the winds wisht.'"

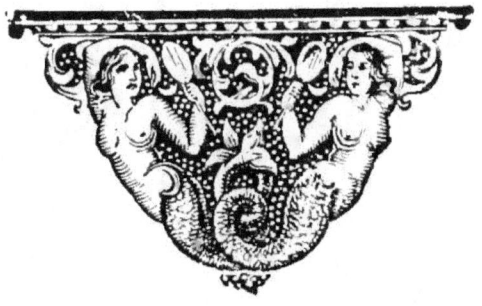

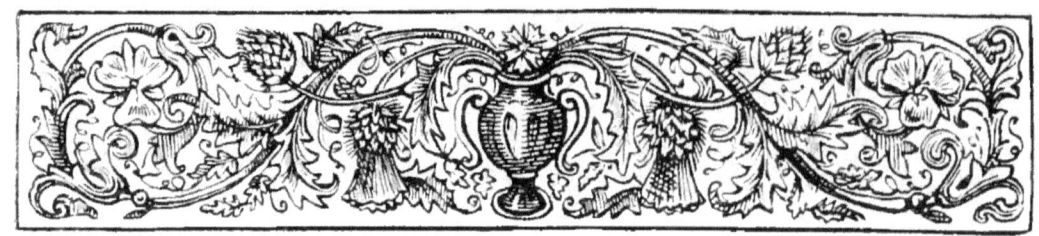

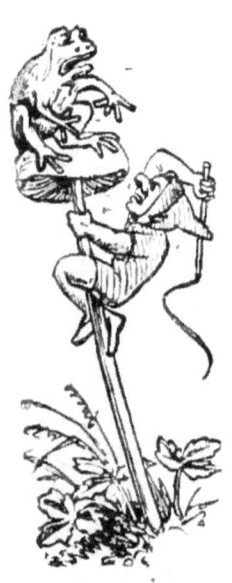

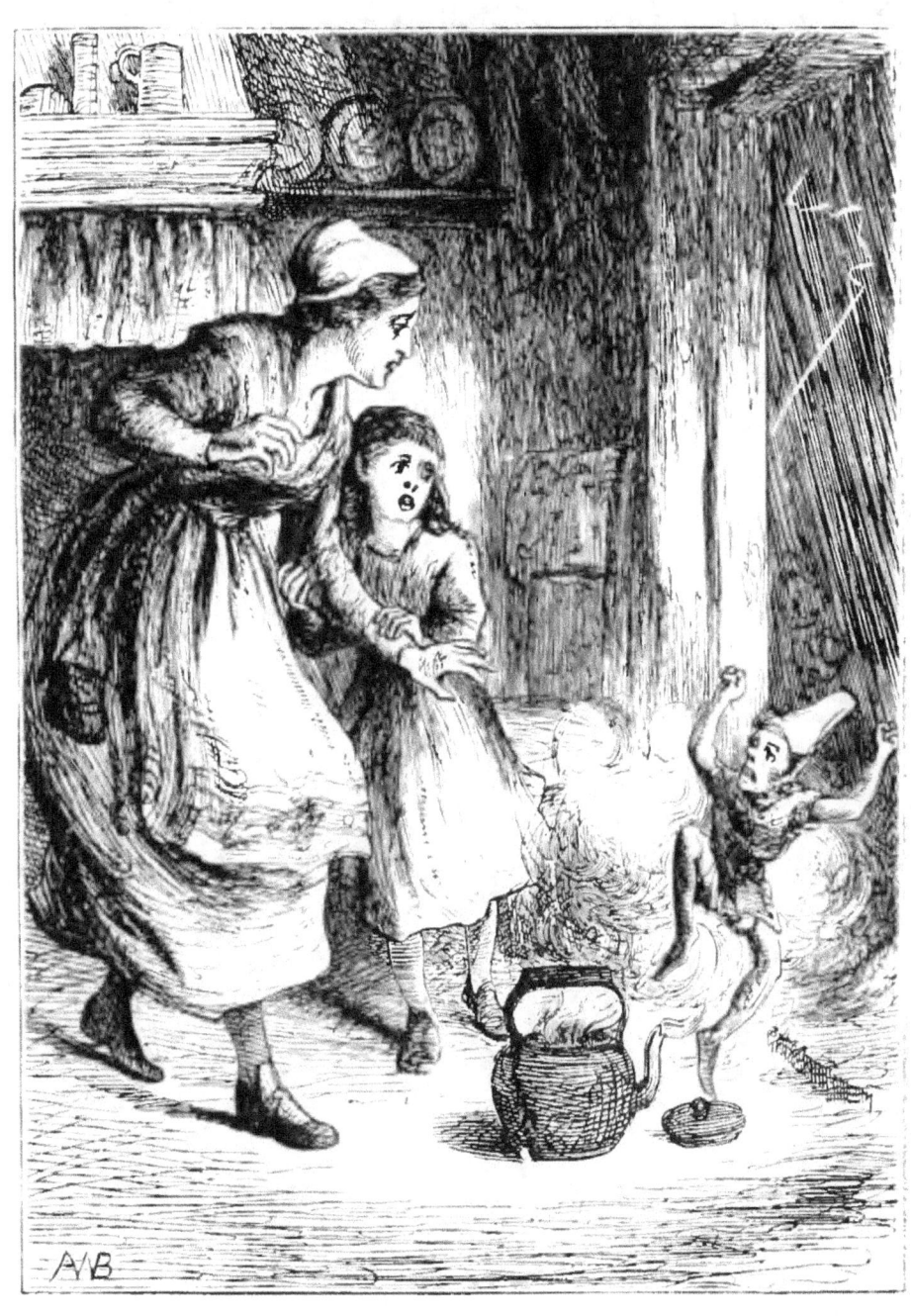

"Out jumped a little man with green teeth and a tall green hat."

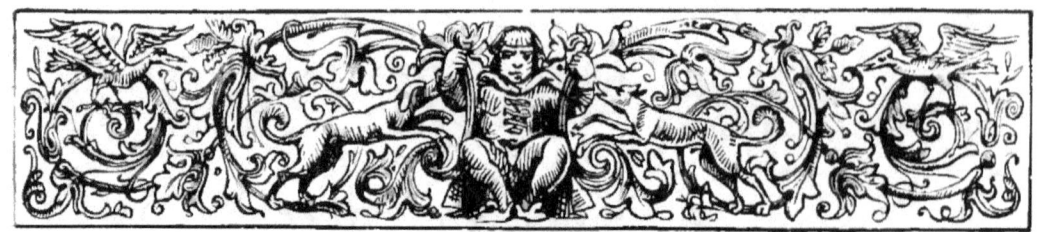

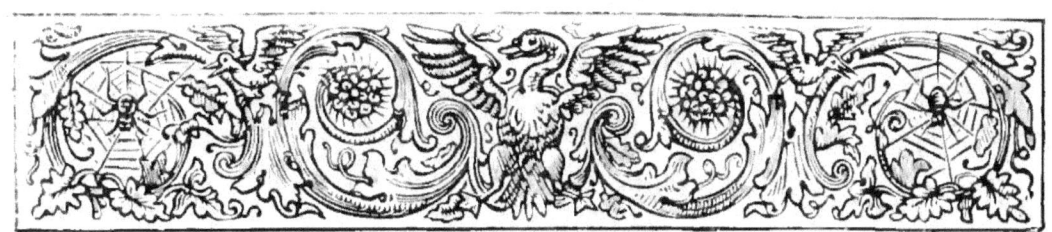

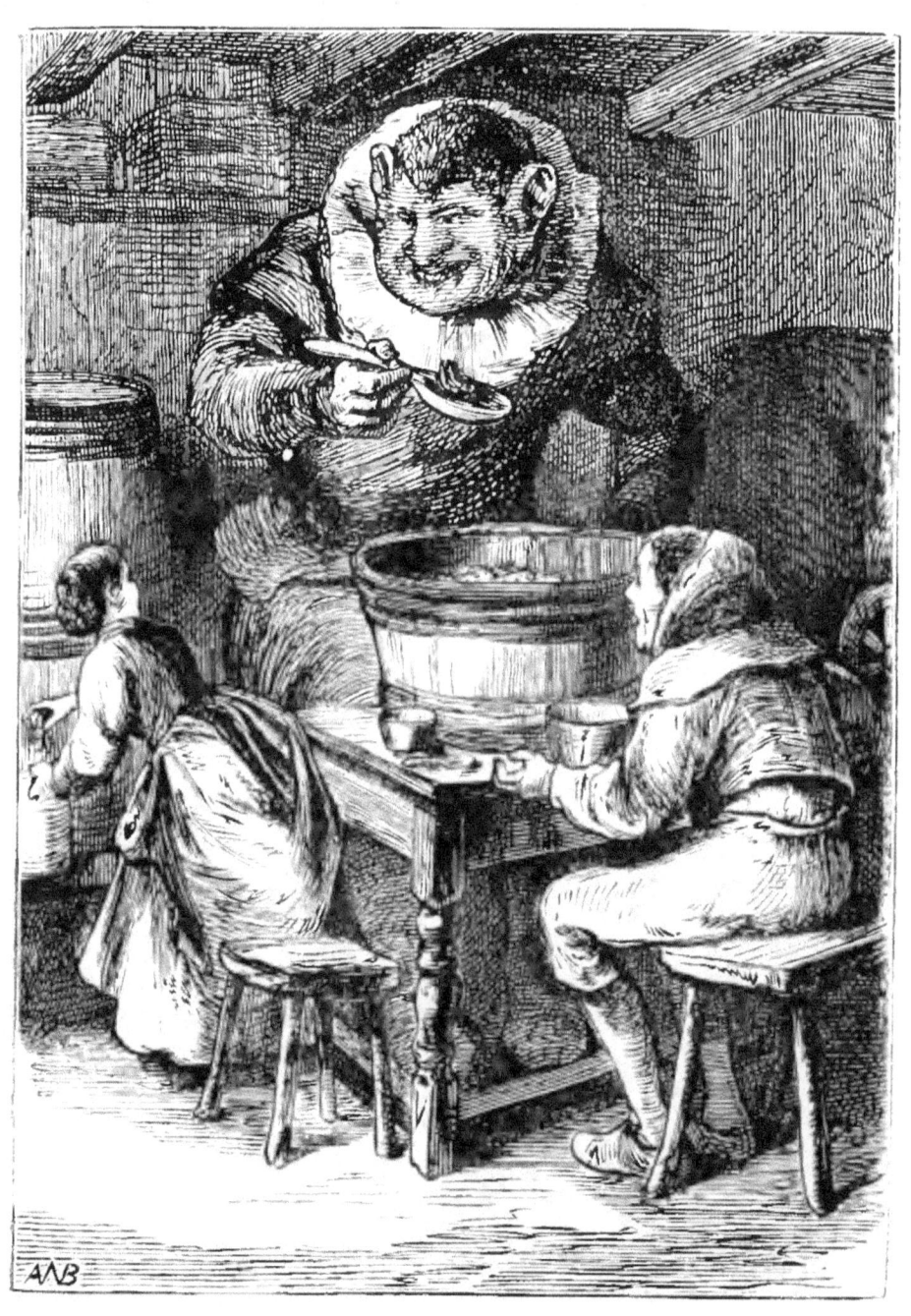

"*What frugality! What a housewife!*"

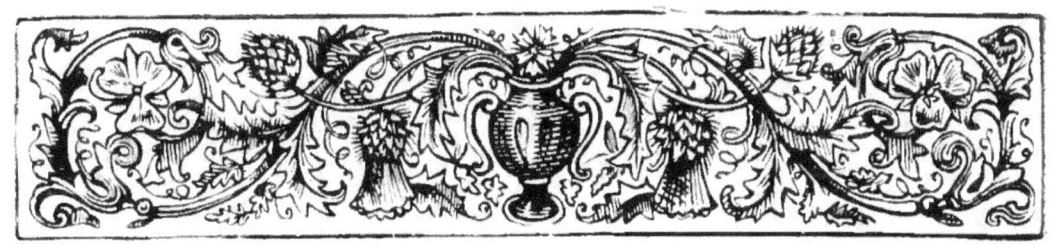

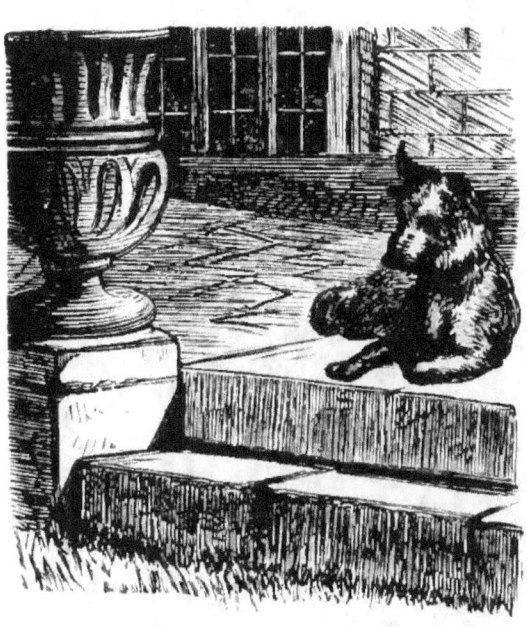

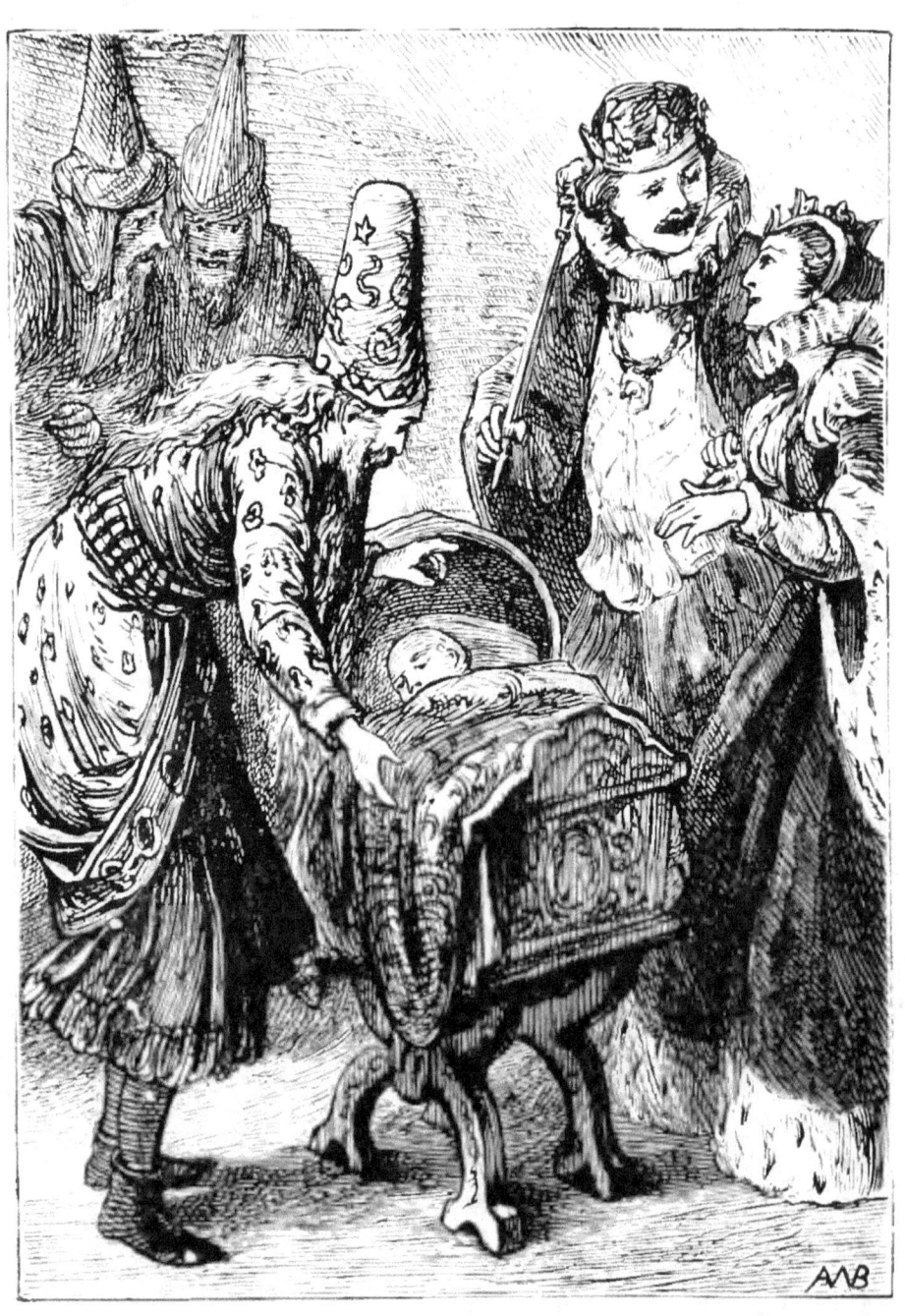

"*The godfather magician advanced to the cradle and said, 'My gift is this.'*"

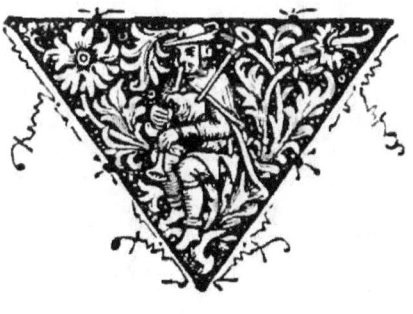

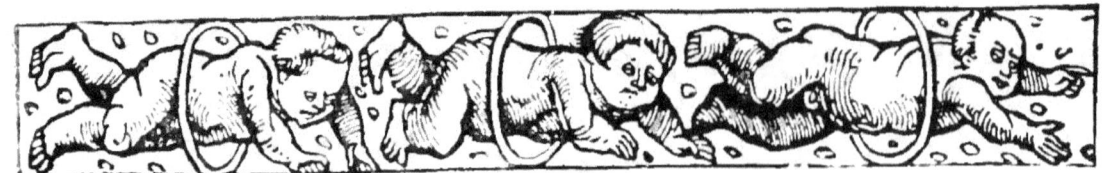

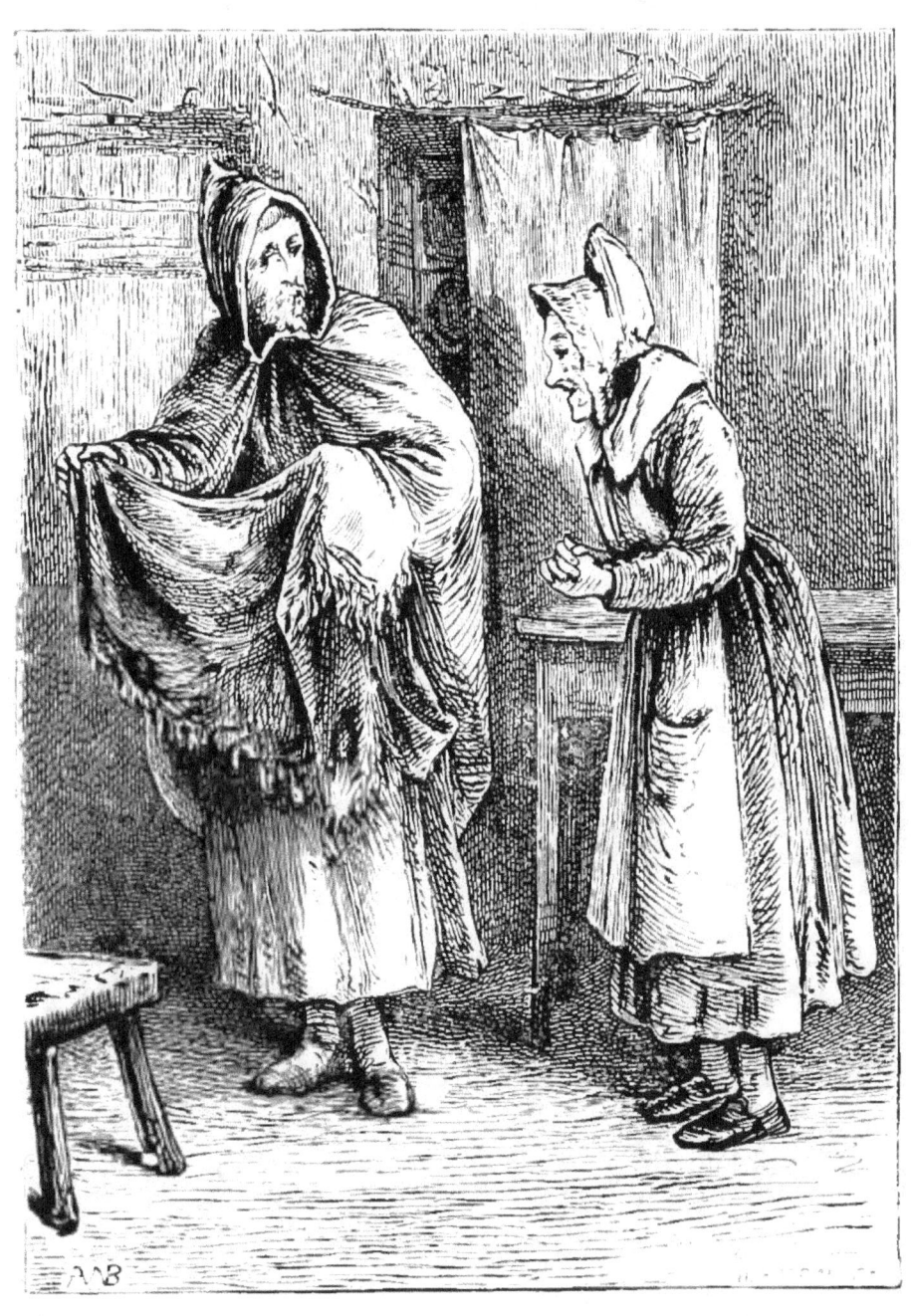

"*It's not so good as it has been, but there's warmth in it yet, and it cost a pretty penny when new.*"

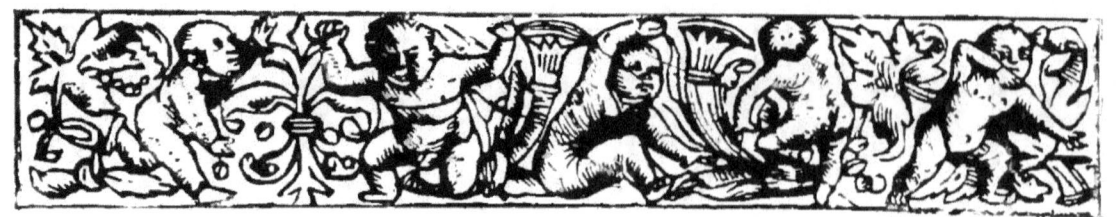

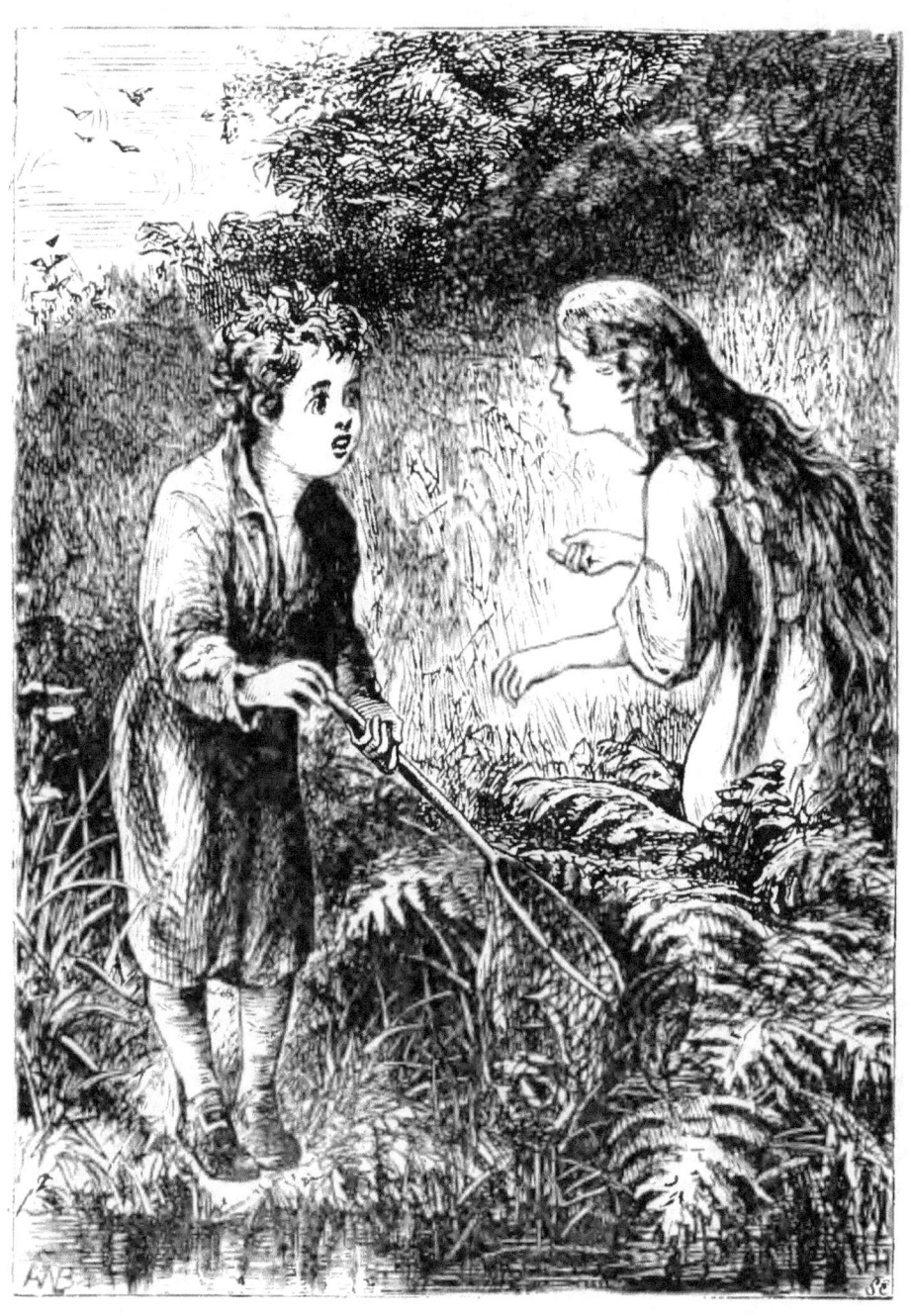

"She was dressed in dark green, and from her knees downwards she was hidden by the clumps of fern."

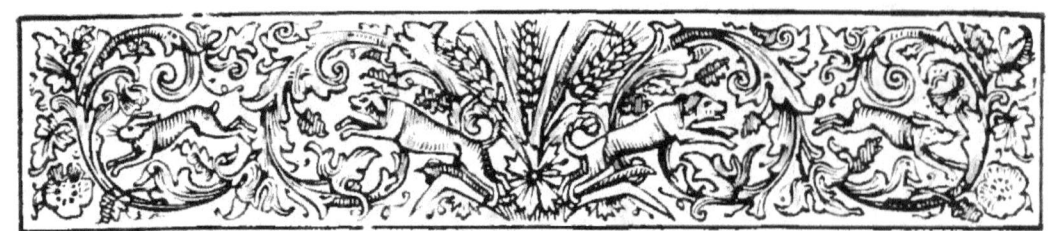

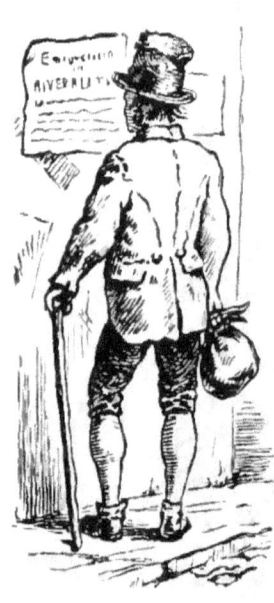

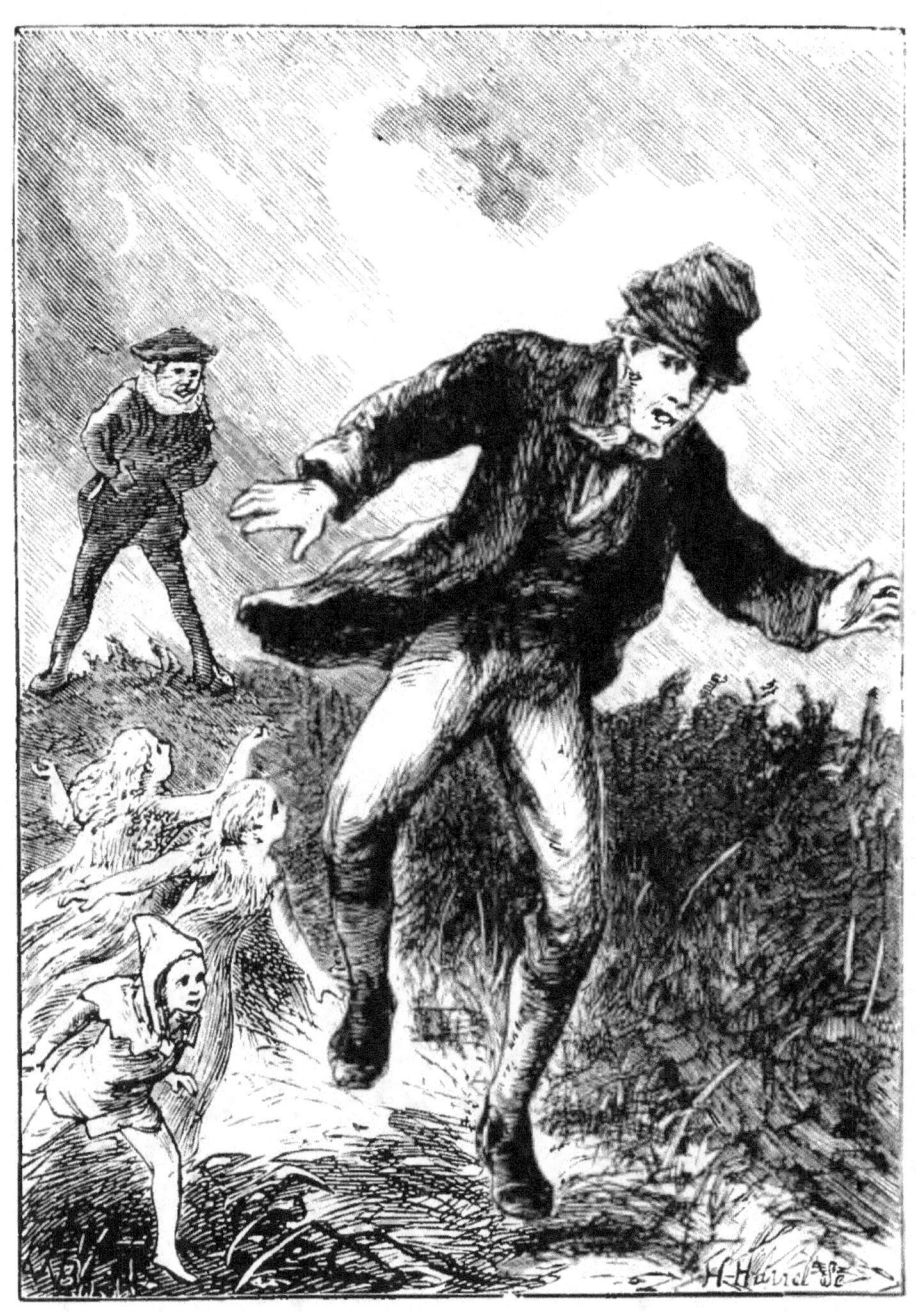

"*The fairies drove him over the ditch, and through the prickly furze-bushes, and he danced away.*"

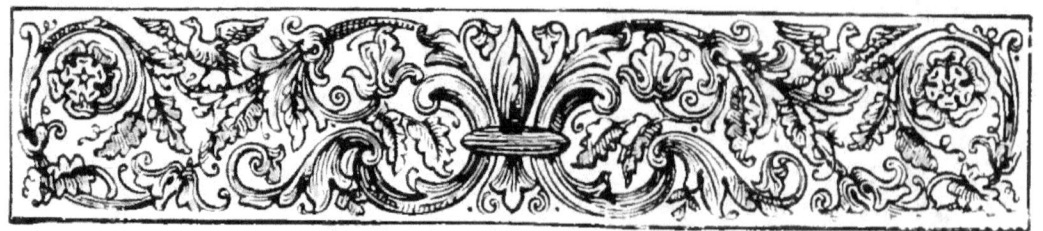

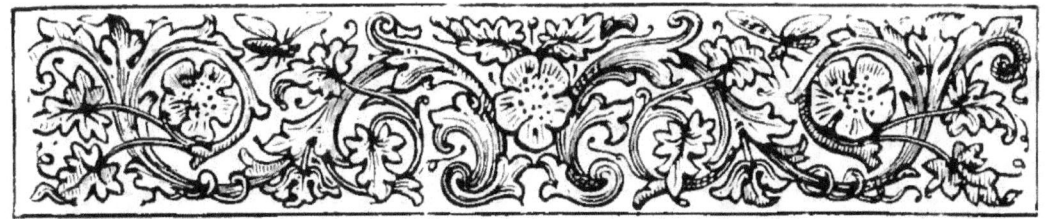

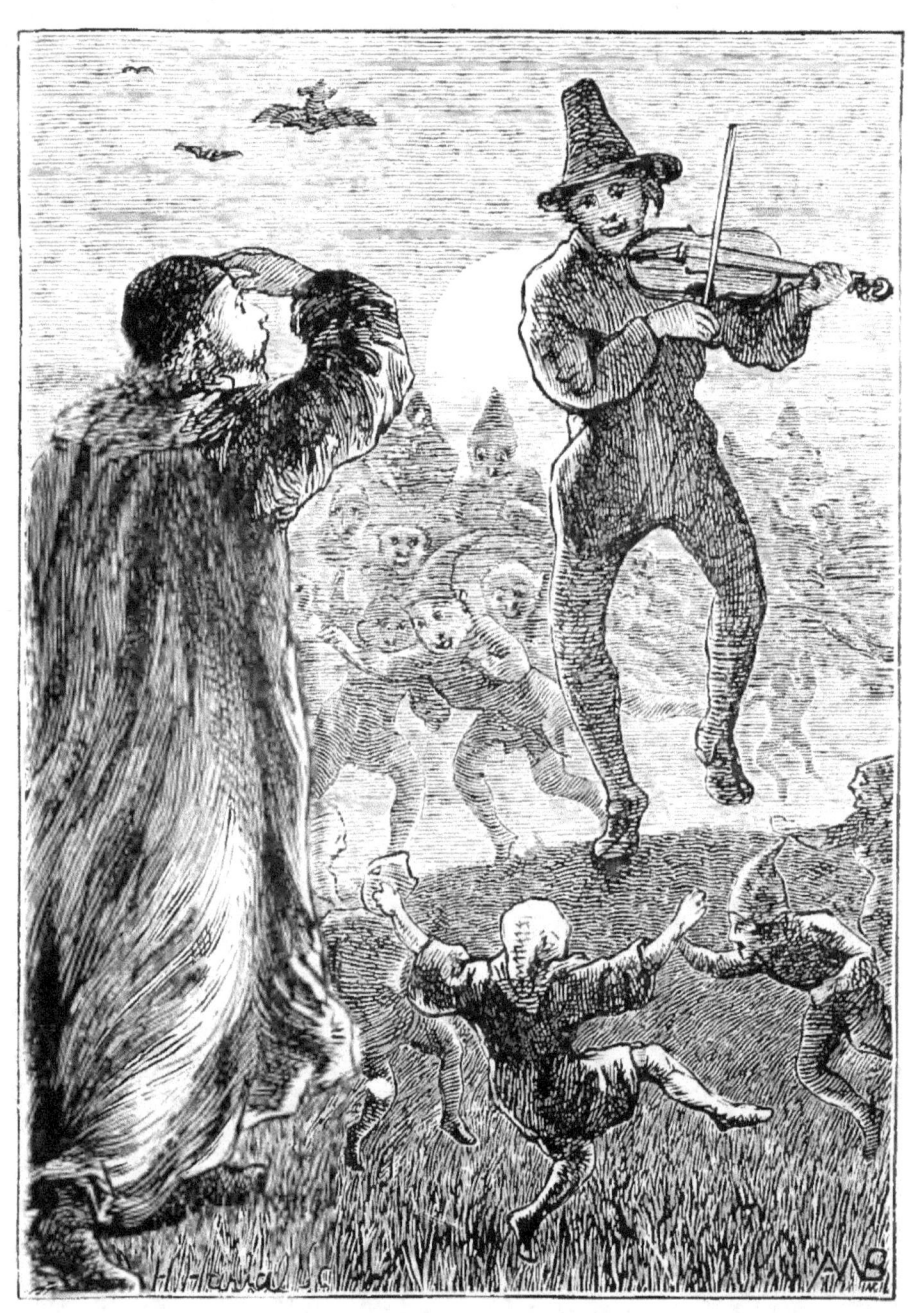

"*The moon shone out, and in the middle of the ring they saw Limping Tim the fiddler.*"

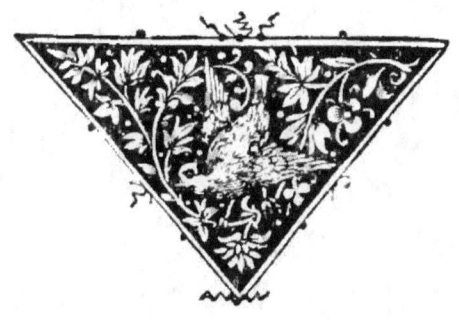

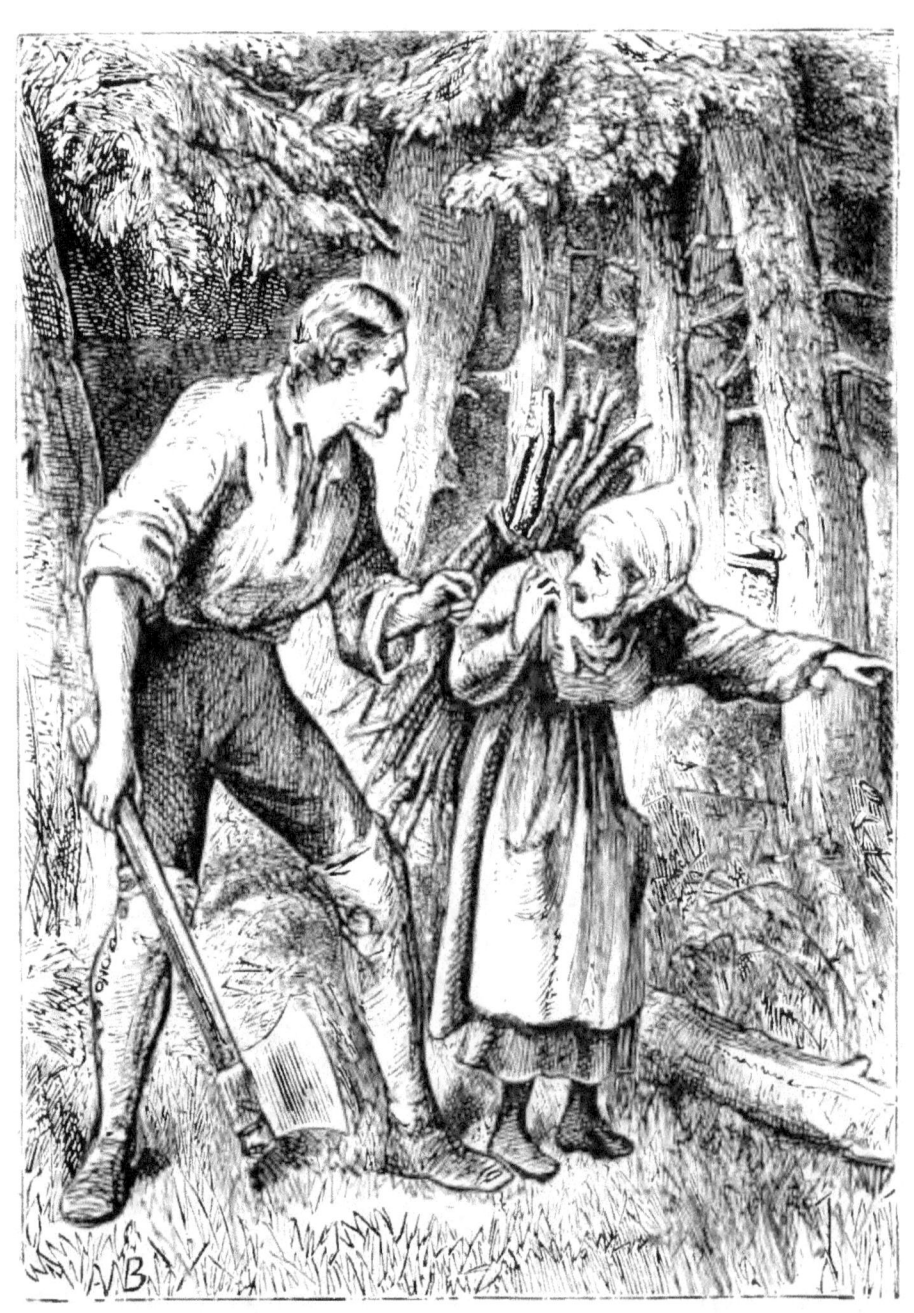

"'Listen,' said she, 'he shall not treat you as he has treated others.'"

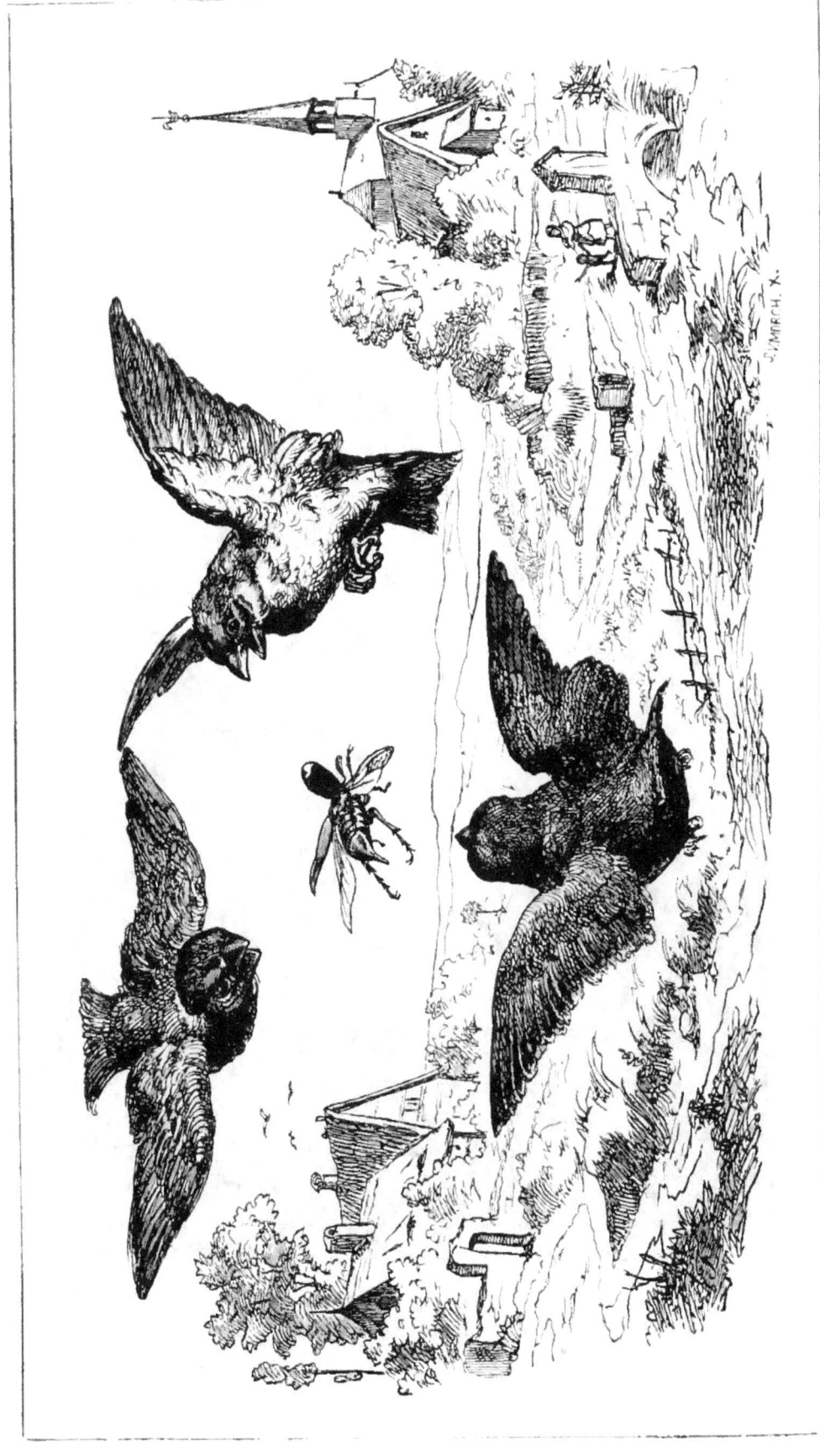

"*From three sides they hemmed him in, crying, 'Which of us told you?'*"

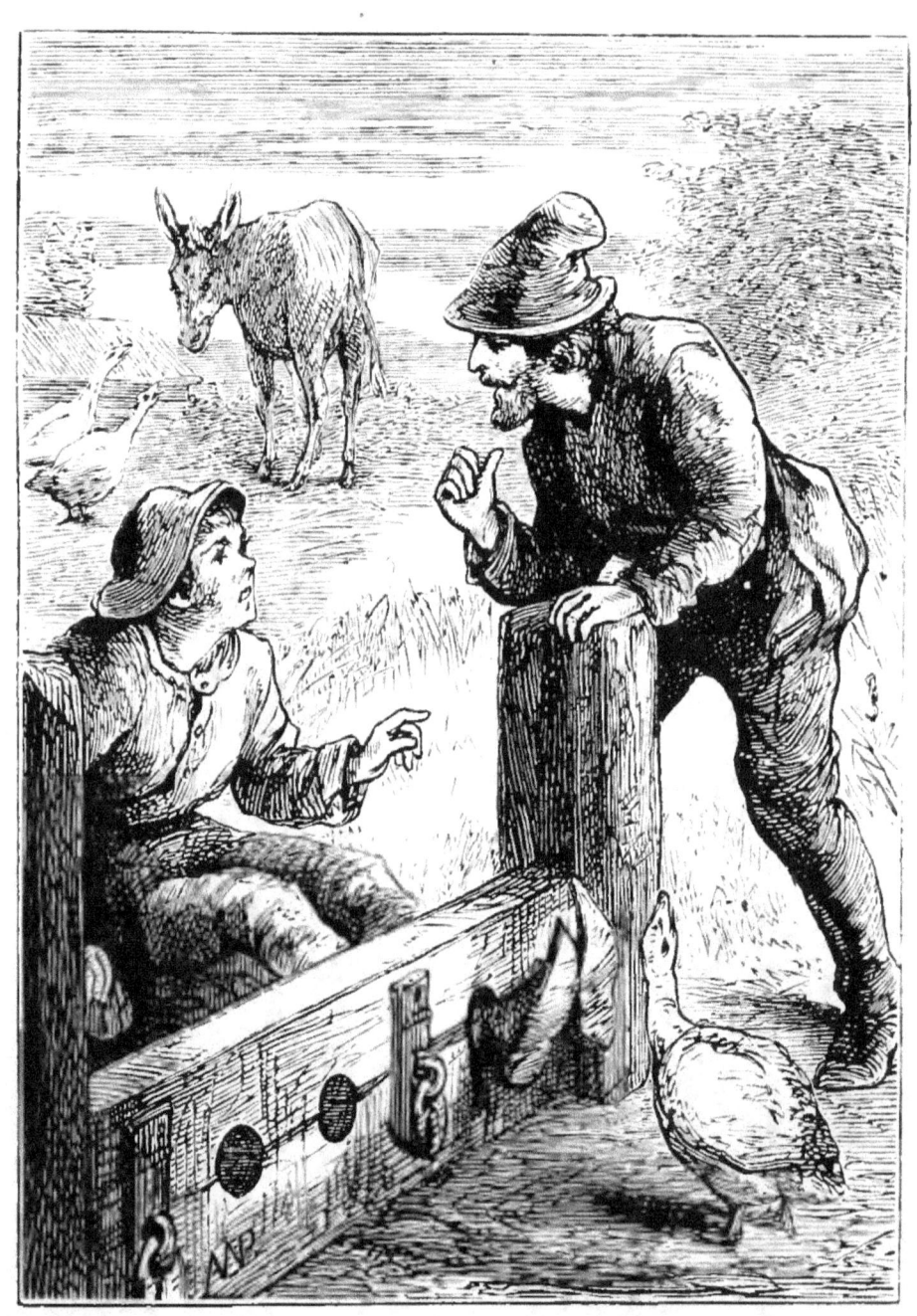

"*The Knave hurried up to the village green, where his friend sat doing penance for the theft.*"

www.ingramcontent.com/pod-product-compliance
Lightning Source LLC
Chambersburg PA
CBHW082224220526
45470CB00010B/3294